Thoughts

Of A

Lover

REDEFINED

By B.J. Carmichael

Thoughts of a Lover Redefined
Copyright © 2020
ISBN: 978-0-578-66483-5

Credits
Editorial: Carla DuPont
Cover Design: Garrett Myers

ACKNOWLEDGEMENTS

The third go 'round and it's been a journey... I appreciate everyone from the crossing guard to the stripper at the gentlemen's club! My family, extended family, friends, everybody who continued to ask, "What's next? We're ready to read more." To the people who shared their feelings with me about the feelings I shared with them and the people who financially, mentally, and emotionally supported... it felt good to know you were there even if I wasn't! The road may or may not be smoother with the continuation of this process to progress. We never know, we just have to keep it PUSHIN' PIMPIN' and ROLLIN', holding what we got and knowing when to fold. Stand tall calling the bluff of all the ones against the brand, the plan, and protocol of being SOCIETYSFINESTIAM... everyone will forever be in my heart. Love will always be felt while you're here because when you're gone... it's just a memory!

Thoughts

Of A

Lover

REDEFINED

7:56 a.m.

Sick and tired of the sick and tired!
Get up and grind!
Product...produce revenue
Get inside your mind...
From the left to the right brain
Connect mane,
If it's 10% that you use
It's 90 left for you to abuse
Pain...
Beat it out of your membrane
Break that hold...
Become the lover
The fighter
The independent of the whole...
Heap of the dreamer
The overachiever
The pass believer
The 'I need to see the plus throughout the minus'
The divide
Multiply
Whatever it takes to find it
The sum...
Go and get you some...
It's yours...
The ratio of what belongs to you is greater than
what does not
You are the source
The choice
The devotion
The lifestyle is motivated upon your contact
The comeback... 'cause there is one

Is the proof to you...
Nothing in this world can stop you from doing you
Except you
Pursue
Follow
Stay on a path...
Sometimes you have to navigate other roads
It is what it is
These are the facts!
Roll with that...

Aggressively Calm

I flip flop and serve those who don't know shit
Invoke knowledge to your horizon with the right
stroke of the stick
In the presence of love, with about 36 ounces of
pure lust
On a scale, from one to ten...
The old school triple beam weighs it in
When emotions surpass that so called playa stat,
Pimpin' rules change and you simply can't get that
playa back
Listen Linda... sit your fine, black ass down!
Daddy's not here to be lollygagging around
Bobby Brown that ass with every little step I take
Bobby Bouche'
Yeah...yeah...yeah...yeah...
You need some water
Yeah...yeah...yeah...yeah
I got it for you

All-in-All

Rolling through the process you will be left with battlefield scars that you tell long stories about later on in life... Loving thoughts of memories from the ones you just had to let go of will be the reason you know how much you can stand for, 'cause you just can't stand no more... Progress comes with A LOT OF pain. Things that change and knowledge that is gained typically isn't appreciated until it's referenced at a later time... All-in-all, stay about your grind.

All Together Now

I love it how you like it... my preference is slow
do'...
It gives me and the putty tat time to get to know
more
Deep conversations about the feelings inside
Aggravating the nerves and severing ties
See, I claim to be daddy's finest from
#SocietysfinestIAM
And baby, your body is mine and I, just don't give a
damn
What time it is...
How tired you is...
I'll compromise some
But
I need my fills...
What it is, is this
King ding-a-ling don't take no shit!
Wit' a twist...
I'm the cocaine addiction
I'm the mofo reason these duck ass lames, names
be missing
Forget to even acknowledge the outside world
I make it my mofo business to protect you gurl
The reason you get sick when, Mother Nature
makes you miss this dick
The entire time they calling you bad and boujee
because outside of the movement ain't no need to
entertain these bitch made groupies

Fuss wit' these dick riding ass hoes
I guarantee they can choose all they want
Can't say they have had the opportunity
To feel the man of steel peel organisms out of their
asses like David Copperfield
Big Dick Magic is my stage name
Your body is the stage frame
Sound check wit' the moans and screams
No soundproof booth can rearrange the volume
from that A-1 head game
So when I say I love it
How you like it
But
My preference is slow…
That's mainly for me to note the way back home
'cause waist deep I'm 'bout to go…
#SocietysfinestIAM act like ya know

Anything Is Possible If You Both Want It...

By all means, if it can be salvaged... save it. If you feel like love is still breathing under the pile of bullshit, clean and rebuild.

If the light still flickers in your ticker... flip her and long stick her.

If there is life left to still live and it's not dead energy... revitalize and live!!! All these things have to be presented on both ends of the stick to work... if it's to work. #SocietysfinestIAM

Aten-Hut

I see how and I appreciate the sight of...
I continue to chase greatness in spite of the haters.
I continue to give because of the data...
Information held maliciously sets a bad taste...
That ain't my flavor.
I refuse to abuse the power I have for a lame ass recipient.
Imma teach anybody who's trying to receive this gift.
Shift lifestyles quicker than a whiff of fresh air...
The better the breath
The better air
The better your health
The better is there...
For your satisfaction
Your enjoyment.
#SocietysfinestIAM is the army
Responsible for fundamental deployments.

1 Of A Few Interludes

Wake up next to the love of your life and make
sweet n' sour love like blending shrimp fried rice.
Get nasty and add some egg "drop" soup.
Stir fry that ass
like steamed broccoli and carrots.
Feast upon each other!

Bar-B-Que Love

Kool aid,
Chocolate cake,
A plate of mashed potatoes,
Corn bread,
Stuffing, and
Just because I need some veggies,
A side of collard greens.
I've just described the sweetest, thickest woman
Back yard bar-b-que smelling like hickory...
Finger licking good.
5'5" she stood.
6' in the hood.
She's standing grounds other women wish they could.
We need that.
Believe that...
How can a man stand alone without a woman to give feedback?
That's a lack of proper education. Understand that woman is part of the destination... Realize together with a real community there will be NO NEED for outside representation,
But back to my perception of this perfect identification of...
Love and bomb ass unheard of...
Pleasure from all aspects of the game. Knowing who I am
You know she's destined to aim...
From the top to the bottom

That is law!
Beast, what u thought?

Beating The Odds

As seemingly easy as it may look,
Nothing comes organized off top.
It takes a car and
a couple of thousand miles
before it's truly broken in.
The wind...
That just feels so perfect...
Went in sooo many directions before it calmed
down.
Check the stats as you go and record mentally
The cons and set in stone the pros...
Let the sun shine,
As it pleases upon your life.
Clouds fade grey, blue, pink, or green.
That air is still precious so, breathe...
Sing,
Happy feelings until you feel happy feelings.
Choices on whether to stay or go,
Or say yes or no...
Decide and let it flow.
Just always have a plan and always know...
You gave as much as you had.
You took and spared
Looked and tried not to get mad.
Even if you did get sad,
That's just because you're really tired
and that... is that.

Brains & Brawn

Brains and brawn
Spawn a hell of an experience to the soul.
Having the physical ability
to perform different activities
then have the nerve
to mentally stimulate agility unknown...
Such a gift when you can express yourself
in double form.
Out of the norm... sometimes a double standard.
Use both to its capacity...
Wise enough to know the strength you behold
Sets standards higher against those who know no
better.
Strong enough to use your wisdom gracefully for
those who've never,
been entertained by a brain with brawn and a
brawn with brains...
Intimately controlling the game with simple
gestures within the same...
Scope...
Hold a grasp so firm,
Melting and they can't believe it's not butter.
Wouldn't even leave if you suggested it,
At your own will them respecting it...
Well rounded and compounded with...
Brains and brawn.
Something truly missed
So rock,
rock on.

Build The Legacy

A house, a spouse, a couple of muscle cars... that's
the dream.
Comfortable recliner, a designer prancing around
cooking...
Just antagonizing the inner beast to break free are
the goals.
Looking out of windows...
Yes the kids are causing a ruckus in the yard...
YES!
In "their" yard.
How perfect would that be?
Amongst the normal issues,
Happiness is just what you will see.
Paying no mind to the ignorant...
Stumbling over the innocent...
Too caught in the given
the evil is irrelevant.
Your own little world where
the dollar is endless.
You've made it to the top,
Just waiting on God to finish it.
These are the dreams individuals have.
The reason some get up and create their own path.
There is nothing like being accomplished by your
own math.
Build the legacy,
It's up for grabs!

Canopy Fantasy

Millions in the ceiling,
Puddy tang on a canopy...
Midnight smash,
Skeeting oil paint on a satin sheet.
Dousing scorching flames on a dame as she dances
for me...
Do it on the snicker
She thicker than a leather seat.
Softer than a cotton ball, tighter than a sealed jar.
Don't know what she did but it's concealed like it's
against the law.
Carrying weapons of mass destruction
As I unbutton her soul on the road to yellow...
Off to see the wizard as she tells me how her heart
is shattered.
I can only give you three wishes,
so please miss me with the fairy tales.
Always keep it real,
love her hard,
heal her nightmares.
#SocietysfinestIAM will always be there.

Captivating Aura

Ripple in the wave,
Ice cream and chocolate.
Butt-naked woman,
sweeter than honey drips.
Feed me lady,
I'm licking you from the nip...
Like riding 285,
your curves require a super grip.
Pressing on the gas,
accelerate deeply into your heart.
Speeding through your mind,
emotions fall right apart.
Hazard lights flash...
CRASH, BAM, and BOOM!!!
#mythoughtsyourfeelings
consumed in the womb.

Celebrate Regardless

Champagne forever
toasting to sex appeal etc., etc., etc...
I would literally wait on you forever,
a lifetime.
I really want to continue working with you during
the trying times...
Am I the fool you've been blessed with?
Do you feel like you're that special someone and
I'm just the next kick?
Emotional skies
shower us with the cries
from the torment we both may feel inside.
I tried calling but,
got no answer...
to the world, I lied.
I portrayed the player pimpin' savior faire...
Cadillac dippin',
iced out flippin',
big bank holdin',
hide how much I care.
The reality is real and everything fake tries to
dictate how you're supposed to live out there.
A-t-alien,
extra-terrestrial,
monosyllabic,
pertaining to the bull of shit
left for you to pull and pick things to get you sick.
The regular basic muthafuckers...
Am I clear?
I need above average,
like Nola Simone, in she's gotta have it.

Sexual fanatic with the means to be free.
Sapiosexuality intriguing to thee...
Spiritual guidance like,
lead yee to me.
I lace up my flip flops and keep it pushing in these streets.
Let my soul bleed bay-bee...
Two shots to the heart from the 1800 sliver.
High hoe feel ya,
yadda...yadda...yadda...
As the liquid instills the,
I don't...
fuck wit...
YOU!
'Cause I know how I get down and
All my,
love is,
TRUE.
I'll still wait a lifetime
or
until God gives me another lifeline
because you just refused your blessing 'cause you ain't
in
your
right
mind...
#SocietysfinestIAM & I ain't lying.

Chasing That First

You're definitely were one of a kind. I've attempted
to find your strength in others,
Well, good, they may have been but your equal
they will never amount to...
They say you can't have just one, I beg to
determine otherwise.
No two are alike and that's just how I feel.
I should have just left it there while it was real!
Now I'm addicted to myself
Just so I can say I can feel.
This life is so short and you just don't notice it
until...
Something diminishes over time.
Take it for what you want, but Coca-Cola has made
me lose my mind.
I need one.

Choices U Make

U know when... I'm quite sure u do.
But any who,
u have that moment and just can't let it go...
U know that I tried to tell u so!
Before it got too much to handle.
In all aspects of the matter,
it ain't nuttin' to deal...
U just more so on, I just want to chill.
Want to be real with those who trill in return...
Those who understand and recognize the value,
who cut their own right hand before they let it
burn.
I, I, I'm just saying!
Y, y, y u playing!
No answer is needed.
I completely see it...
U and I are different breeds.
From the nails on our toes,
to the wrinkles in our noses,
to the split ends and however far it goes.
See, see, and see me!
And, and, and u...
Were cool and compatible from friends to boo.
Now u just bae, and I'm caution...
Sitting here waiting to go Dutch 'cause I ain't
paying.
U list the lost and I lost the list...
Now pen n' pad jotting down some mo' righteous
shit.
Bad, bitch please.
I can agree.

One more week and a change of degree...
I'm sho' gone show u,
u must not know 'bout me.
These are the breaks when u renege on the
coochie tree...
U should have never left me...
Cunt-inuosly,
hot and horny.
Peace.

Confessions

Confessions of a naughty librarian, telling you when after the fact. Multiple orgasms back-to-back... Shush you with every stroke... Noise control, wanting to scream from every poke. (no Facebook) Attitude so innocent, until you check out and get into it. Then she nasty! Ask me have I followed the instructions the way they say carry every act out. Wow, so knowledgeable about your literature. She says, (not at all, just the ones that knock down walls.) Good lawd... Librarian, you the naughtiest of them all.
#king #beast

Corner Pocket 8-Ball

She said her favorite game was pool.
That's where she mastered the art of handling that
stick...
Call her "Que Ball" for short
Cause she aims and busts balls quick.
Listen to her lingo...
Calling and sinking each and every pocket.
Her words were,
"I love to clear the table,"
As I was chalking my stick.
Getting ready to drop it...
She had things all laid out.
Ready to be queen of billiards.
Her words were,
"I treat my king as if he dominates.
Anything he needs
I'm the woman he nominates."
This conversation leads to a lifetime of corner
pocket bank shots...
Combination straight up the middle.
If this was a tournament...
I'd have to slick put all my bets on this winner.
Loser racks,
damn baby stacked.
Handle that stick like a professional,
busting balls back-to-back.
Climax like,
take that,
and that...
She calls

"8 ball off all walls and slow in the side."
#SocietysfinestIAM plant my feet and just glide.

Cuffing Season

She kissed my lips,
so I kissed hers back...
She caved into my chest shortly after that.
I held her close,
I mean it is cuffing season...
The brisk air seeped through the window and I felt
a reason...
A reason to love her real good right at that
moment.
She returned the gesture and now there's another
component added to the plot.
She begged me to stop after two or three rounds...
I wondered, *what happened* as if I didn't lay it
down.
She said to me, "I need you in my life for more than
just one night."
I said back quickly, "With all that's going on in my
life, I'm not sure if this would be right...
Hesitant to leave, she kissed me one last time and
since she's left...
It's been even more difficult to breath.
"Why me?"

Damsel In Distress

Every woman needs a superhero,
A nymphomaniac...
Damsel in distress
Depressed
Talking, "Come get the cat..."
It don't know how to act
Wit a mean spirit,
A menace,
She needs a chief to come put his teepee in it,
She wants me to be Navajo,
Imma Poke-her-hontas.
She needs a superhero who can show her
something...
More than the egotistical...
Eat,
Beat,
and skeet it...
She needs a king who can do things like,
Treat and feed it.
Can you see it belongs to thee?
Beholder of the stroke,
Which is me...
As I begin to hold her,
She begins to be...
All in her comfort zones, with a real OG...
Moving fast forward to the structured process.
She has a plan to be on top of the peace for the
king and his nest...
Home laid like a palace,
All bills paid...

Baby done fucked around and made some
homemade lemonade.
So I...
Play my part even tighter than before.
Imma man,
A greedy man so,
You know I want more...
Put mo' ingredient into the pot!
Playa like myself keep the stove good and piping
HOT!
Plot!!!
Plan!!!
Strategize!!
I'm speaking very mild mannered but the ultimate
prize...
Is deep inside your thighs,
I mean eyes...
Forgive me for my luscious ways...
I'd be a cotton picking liar trying to act like I ain't
attracted to that maze...
Of ecstasy
Standing right in front of me.
It's the nature of my soul to connect with intimacy.
Looking into the eyes of my beauty queen...
Rolling down 285,
Solidifying who are the players of this team!

Datway!!!!

That long cold night,
That warm cup of coffee...
Touched with a lil' bit of yak. Something soft,
thick,
Cute, caressing your feelings until you are at ease...
Getting real tempting about this time.
Shaking trying to get a hold of the matter.
It really doesn't matter,
it's gonna happen either way... *Shhhh*...
Whispering, "Sweet dreams."
It's just a late nights/early mornings type of thing.
Work coming up in a few hours
that's the least of the worries.
This work that's in front of you is the complete
focus...
Emotional maintenance comes before everything
and that's law.
I rest my case...

Desired Calories

Life is like a box of chocolates…and you are like a bottle of wine. Putting you together in my life, is like the sweetest and drunkest feeling ever, slated to have a great time. Even as the days grow shorter and night even longer… that's just the message that, pushing time back was meant for intimate sessions. The true test is having the stamina to do you right. As the drift of the thrust eases your tension, you listen to your body talk and your mind blends in with the sentences… as the long night's brisk air turns into sunrise, a chill morning… your soul is ever so heated and prepared to face any challenges that think they are stronger than your rejuvenated soul, body, and horny mind. #societyfinestiam worth every second of your time.

Different Breed

I had to beat her. That's the way she likes for me to treat her... I tried to be nice, she said that didn't please her. I was gentle and she seemed to get bored. But when I beat her, man... she kept asking me for more. I switched it up and everything. Damn near lost her. Pissed me off so bad, I had to assault her. She started telling me things, things you wouldn't believe. Had the nerve to even threaten me... Said I bet not leave. Goodness she's a freak. I mean, I can dig it, too. She likes it aggressive... beating that poo poo. Boo boo a fool. She still calls it making love... I thought it was a fuck... Well, whatever playa...a nut is a nut.
#societysfinestiam

Disconnect Notice

We all do things that we're not supposed to do.
Gratification for being who we chose to be,
Right or wrong, there's no justification,
No judgement passed either,
At least we don't care whether there is or not.
Still the facts remain,
Who's the blame?
Is there a blame?
A route to where it all began?
Was it the elders who told you to go?
For the knowhow and the down fall of the square
ball not being round?
Nope...
At the end of the day we are accountable for the
shit we do...
The judge says,
They can put the drug in your hand but no one can
make you sell it. That was your decision.
You suffer your own consequences...

Don't Ask If You're Not Ready

I have the time if you have the energy. Plenty me,
Worthy of you and your submissive gene.
In those genes,
I'm seeking my beauty queen.
Prissy thing...
attitudes when it's about her king.
Feisty mean...
I love it like I love Mayfield's ice cream.
It's an Atlanta thing...
I love Mayfield's anything.
Know what I mean?
She's like my Mayfield's addiction theme.
Home grown,
Solid business right in between her ears...
Yeah, man I love it here.
Her mind is so sublime like tequila and limes...
I'm tipsy, near drunk in love,
She surfboards the wave enough...
Causing a tsunami she clears the beach
I'm just waiting for that kick back.
You just gotta love that.
She reads me well,
gypsy talking and giving hell.
Don't come for her 'cause she's gonna come to me.
Cumming for me...
Well, that's the catastrophe.
I wanna live, laugh, fuck, and chill.
My baby is my baby, find your own and pay some
bills.
It's happy here...
So believe it ain't no fear.

I have the time if you have the energy to prosper,
dear.

Down, Set, Hut...

Have you ever seen a person so fine, the word 'dime' couldn't even describe them? Just to look into their eyes and try to define them. You couldn't get an answer to none of your thoughts. You try to analyze by the language in the walk. The tone in the talk. The gesture of the face. You know that it's love, but do they think the same way? Do they feel the place being rushed with adrenaline? Do they look at you and say there's my, I will again... put it on the line, the sleeve of my left arm. I will believe you are the one to protect me from the lost ones. The entry to forever. For there will never be an end. Too far from a dime, I'm four quarters in...

Dress For The Day

Been woke since the wee-wee, thinking about
much of nothing.
Thinking about all of something, trying to
appreciate whatever is coming.
I know it has to be great, it's been a struggle for
quite some time now.
Hurricane season isn't just pertaining to the
weather.
It can be fall all year 'round no matter how hot or
cold.
Tank top or sweater...
Betterment, brethren I assure you that it's greater
than disappointing letters and love that failed you.
Appreciative for the lesson that's taught with the
intent to,
open eyes and minds so that you don't continue to
fall victim to,

the plight of your own ignorance.
The plunder of others.
Control your own life! Like no other.

2 Of A Few Interludes

Time moves as fast as you're standing still...
You are actually behind time, even as you move.
So your best bet is to keep up the momentum.
You can't make up for lost time... and you damn
sure don't need to waste the time that's coming...
Because it's not promised to you...
It's a gift you should appreciate.

Epiphany

She was the epitome of freaky, an epiphany to
thee.
Epic in the sense that, searching for anything
better after
was just an epidemic, a strife!
Emotionally draining looking for entertaining acts
of life!
Wife...
She made it her business to be.
Why?
Was she really into me? Is it just a scheme to be,
you know...
What all women aim to see?
The house!
Dog!
Picket fences and a Christmas tree.
Nevertheless though, she gave it her all so
I could be happy and better and wiser and pleased
and in love with her from head to feet.
Sheesh!
She!
Is a beast not me...!
I'm just the king her highness dreams of.
Creams for!
Following my lead for!
Indeed bruh!
She never wants to leave her team fa!
Anything in 'THIS' world.

Boy stooop!
And that's my ego, she gon', put it in motion.
My hero.
In the bedroom because she lets me be me!
But I fucked it up now I, feel like a zero.
Goes to show, high can just as well become low.
Looking for my...
Ready, set, go... Ya know?

Fear Is A Lie That Lives Inside You

We all have had liars tell us this and tell us that... We seemed to believe until the truth reveals itself. Then get upset with the "liar." Guess who the BIGGEST LIAR in the world is though... YOUR FEARS. Your fears will have you believing whole heartedly that you can't or something won't be or happen or you're no good for whatever the case maybe. Reveal the "truth" to your fears. Get upset with yourself for even entertaining that lie and show "fear" that the truth is in you... You can and will.

Fixing Things The Right Way

As I kissed her while she walked through the house, she began to feel erotic and grabbed me firm on my crotch. I poured her a glass and we sat on the couch... Kissing like teenage love birds and talking about the things we need to work out. I knew we'd been a little distracted with trying to make it out of our slump. We still had date nights and partied with the couples and fronts... We talk every day without missing a beat. It was still a strain on our relationship and it was getting too deep. I just had to save the most important obligation in my life. So I hung a mistletoe in every underpass, setting up to wet her camel toe. Connection is key, Imma make sure I'm in possession of the master. Mistletoe is the setup as she looked up with laughter.

A Fraction of the Cost

She calls me dark and lovely, I call her... my kookies
and kream. We blend so smoothly that, ruffles are
only a potato chip.

A processed image... scrimmage, time to end the
confusion. You and your team must... recognize
who the FUCK we are.

For $19.99 plus tax, mofo you can own your very
own copy of the video. This the type that won't be
televised, bootlegged, or duplicated unless...

All access has been granted, understand it. Dammit
I hate to even do it to you this way... but um,
kookie has a fetish and myself, I have a fetish for
kookies and kream.

The game so solid that, I can charge anything and
do nothing and I still come out on top...

She calls me dark and lovely but it's not for what
you see up top. That's some facts for that ass...

Kookie seriously loves kream and
#societysfinestiam loves the same damn thing...

For Breakfast

Rose petals to give a little color to the seduction
and some wine to ease the excitement of it all.
No candles, baby u already on fire.
I like the look of enthusiasm your body sends me...
Just ready to endure all that comes your way.
It's not like it's been a while since the last time
either.
U're just so energetic... I see your plot.
Never gon' stop,
Never gon' stop,
Never gon' stop, is the plan
Dancing like this can surely enhance the trance.
We don't even use the fruit for what it's meant for!
Have we been tricked from the get go.
Same thing with the honey... it was never meant
for biscuits.
It was made to sweeten up this stick as u sipped
the dipped glazed off the tip...
Woooooow smack them hips. #SocietysfinestIAM
woke up like this.

For Every No, There Is A Yes

I really think she likes me. She made it her business
to let me know who was helping her after me.
It was none of my business or concern. I mean
yeah, she's gorgeous and fine, of course I'd like her
to be mine.
Time and time and time again, we've locked eyes
but...
That was it. It's a sticky situation that I have to
capitalize on very soon if what I think is true.
The opportunity may never present itself again. I
might just have to create an incident. I won't let it
pass me by... no, no, no. Just as long as she can
match my fly.

Get It How You Live

Big ol' thighs drive me crazy,
Soft and tatted, pretty lil' lady.
Do you really care about my feelings on a daily??
Is it more so how I'm feeling?
So you can play with...
My mind,
Time,
Emotions,
What not!
Lying, crying to get me to conform to that bull,
Stop!
This is the issue...
It's more refreshing when I don't have to miss you.
You're there regardless of the circumstance.
Making love to my pain giving life another chance.
Let's dance, I'm talking 'bout really move...
Then let's cruise
I'm talking 'bout really smooth...
Etc.

Good Looks Don't Cook

What you being "fine" got to do with anything?
I saw, I chose, and I conquered.
The comfort of the eye appeal was your benefit,
not mine...
It's complimented with the ideas of your mind. I
shine bright with or without a dime.
Now make it a combo and then and only then will I
take time... To make due of how your issues affect
me.
Do my part to bar any and every thing that thinks it
can inflict harm upon, yeah... I shot the sheriff, his
comrade the deputy...
All his mofo allies for thinking they could fuck with
me... about you,
Shitting me.
Sucka for love? Naw player that's that turned up
pimping, ya see... My stable is mine, now stick
yoself Pretty Tony!
Can you buy that?!
I thinks not. Now look at what ya did girl. I'm all
outta character, all in my mode to beat a mofo...
Get in the car!
I'm too pretty for this... and you too cute for the
drama momma. Knowing I'm a deadly plummer,
laying and busting pipes all up in ya stomach.
Number one stunna with comma after comma...
like a rollercoaster ride, with loops and screams
like **thunder, bam, thunder**.
You and your heart like Trey Songz been through a
fumble... needed to be intercepted because those

plays y'all were calling were highly disrespected...
for the caliber of emotional maintenance you need.
#SocietysfinestIAM #king #beast so therefore
I have no other option but to succeed. In love, life
and prosperity. I ain't playing **NO GAMES**...

Champagne for the occasion, you fucking with a
man! Understand and overstand that will you?
So being fine is a plus, this is true.
But if you ain't shit... what the fuck are good looks
gonna do?

Gooooo Figure

Inactive activities,
they just be killing me.
A thoroughbred for a thoroughbred
I seek equality.
Dollar for dollar, pound for pound, I beat the
system G.
Fake love there's just too much of, that's just the
agency...
Call me radical, outlawed disciple.
Reference from the bible, but the one and only idol
is MY God.
Let's not get it twisted... I seek undisclosed misses,
no one knows how we get and it's all good.
Watch the birth of our nation... compelling in all
aspects from demonstrations of,
least to greatest financial empowerment.
Self-sufficient rules of engagement that will still
unify some major playa shit.
I could go on but, you get the picture... it's on you
to develop the images in HD... Go figure.

Hold It Steady

Tempo, temporarily, changes temperatures. Beat it like they need it, then proceed to control the heated climate until a cold front lingers over those cold emotions.

Then repeat it for however long it takes to break that silence of... into the more respectable, submissive rite of passage.

Savage... using the tempo to tempo-rarely changes a hostile temperature to a conveying point-of-view, through... emotional maintenance.

How We Met

It all started from an intimate hug at a gas station...
We began conversing during our lunch breaks, she
worked up the street from where I worked. I used
to roll her weed while she pleased me orally. We
stayed going out to eat, weekly expansion of the
mind as we ran through the city. She was very
pretty and no matter how much I told her... She
never believed me.

She would leave me at the drop of a dime! Saying
things like, I'm too good and it would never work.
She ain't shit and she don't want to hurt... me. In
one breath, she would tell me she loves me and
wants us to be, badly. In another, fucked me how I
wanted then wouldn't call back. Time would always
pass and we'd be somewhere catching up... Like
yesterday wasn't months ago, like it was forever
just us.

I had always moved on but when she popped back
up, I'd play the role with the newbie. Treat her like
a groupie as if I wasn't one in the same. This dame
just had what I wanted and honestly what I wanted
was nothing serious just something stable to
maintain. Everybody else had plans for my life,
wanting to become my wife and I, myself, just
couldn't swallow that nice... Even though I

portrayed to Miss Little Undecided that that life suited us right.

Here we go again fucking through the night. Rolling through the streets gazing at the lights! Keeping conversations short, being reckless at the sight... We both had some issues that just kept us from walking right. I figured that's why we ended up being so tight. I didn't judge her, she never judged me. We just filled the time for what each other needed to see.

Can't help but wonder what it was she saw in me. She could have had who she wanted, I saw that through the mystery machine. Niggas would hold conversations with me not knowing (at least that's what I thought) we were shooting the breeze. She confronted me about a chick who gave me a set of house keys... The world was truly a small space when it came to her and me. Some niggas would talk behind my back to the other women trying to fix up a nasty lie.

No one knew what was going on, even though threats came from both sides... We had plugs like no other, being Kool was really suicide. We didn't give a rat's ass, parked cars in lots and smashed in unmarked luxury. Escaping the reality is how she was loving me... Wanted a baby and all, well usually it's when I'm knee deep in her walls. It was all Kool as summer became the winter. Another season from the cold to now, spring... Years flew by back-and-forth we were doing the same things.

SHIT got old but familiar so it had to be broken...we always kept the truth present no secrets and doors open. Like a temp service if it was a position to be filled, it was no problem no matter how much short notice... Right now seasons are changing, we'll see what comes of this life that's dangerous... To be continued... (Temp service)

3 Of A Few Interludes

What I appreciate the "moist", I mean most out of the entire series?

Is that she never let that bread go without no spread.

She never left you hungry or horny for affection, attention, or emotional maintenance.

I Did, I Did

Suffering succotash!!! All that class and a whole
lotta ass...
Pass the cream, suga I think I might just become a
fiend!
You like your coffee dark, baby the blacker the
better...
I am that caffeinated sip you NEED!!! Now open up
and hydrate your soul to the point of no control,
true this is a fact INDEED!
My resume exceeds pleasure, pain, and satisfaction
to gain... Salary desired... It's not a monetary thang.
I came, I sought, and I conquered your heart! You
came, you fought, and you realized what you
thought had you completely at fault.
Never had you had any issues... I know baby, I'm
the shit! Here, you need some tissues.
Anywhoo! It was you that intrigued my mind to
incline the ladder of love aggressively. It was you I
choose to permanently lay next to me...
Blessed to be happily ever after respectfully. In
depth with me, emotional stability you give to me.
So... It's you who's feeding me and me who's
feeding you... Again the truth, so who's really
needing who?

Dilemma Emma

I have a dilemma, Emma...
See, I've been this dude ever since I could
remember.
Sim simma!
Now all of a sudden you want me to erase the *pimp*
pimpa...
Fender bender! It was that very same Kool that
made it so smoove to make love and THEN go out
to dinner...
Trend breaker... So how in the HELL do you think
that will sale...
For me to end that make up... Character shape up!
I'm not asking of you to refuse what you do, if it is
you that make that cake up.
Don't set the fake up.
Being someone you ain't will make this ship sink
with no one there to save us.
Don't make that mistake girl... You really want this
dessert put on reserve, 'cause you feel you deserve
every serving of this Scorpio's delight.
Well, get your weight up!
Imma be there, but baby be fair, with what you
bring to add to the plate, love,
besides the makeup... dilemma Emma,
sim simma.

I Love Me, Too

She texted me, she loved me
and I never sent a reply.
It's not because I don't love
her, I just think her love is a
stipulation, to a lie...
She wants me to deny, my
right to be treated... with the
best love life could give,
something she doesn't have...
Telling me I'm greedy, needy,
selfish... but wants me to give
her the same thing???
Wants all my energy for her
but won't feed the energy so it
can maintain...
The power source it needs to
continue to achieve... the
levels that she needs to
continue to believe.
I'm only human... not a robot
in disguise.
Emotions are real and
everything seems like a lie. So
I...
Have to rejuvenate myself.
Replenish the love that I got
from no one else.
Taking care of me is all I can
do. She texted she loved me
and I'm proving I love me, too.

I Loved Her, Not Enough

I loved her just as far as I could fuck her...
I mean she truly had my heart!!
Especially when those legs were apart. She gave
me what I wanted and I gave her what she never
had.
A real man who destroyed her past and made way
for her future...
I loved her, not enough though, her Cadillac tires
went flat...
I changed all four of them bitches, filled her gas
tank to the 'F' sign, she lost her mind but to me...
It was worth my time. She blew 'til she was blue.
Then she blew some more...
I loved her,
Not enough so much that I controlled her roar. She
lived for my turmoil, my hazards of life.
My, baby
I need you to do this right now. She said she
wanted to be my wife.
I was loving her,
Not enough that she earned a degree higher than
when I met her.
She said at my rate, I would be making her better
for the other feller...
Even if it was true.
A memory of me would always be her truth...
Reason she knew I loved her... not enough.

Beauty In The Broken

I see beauty in the broken. Being that I am the chosen. Hoping one day that I am chosen. Being a beast I'm not withholding. Rolling on anything to preserve the rest of my, everything. Neglecting nothing to appreciate something. The assumption that you don't miss it 'til it's gone maybe true for some. I don't want to be that one to become struck with regret because I wasn't the one. Options are present... But it is you, who are my present... Behold what's in your presence, for it is you that I want to be blessed with. I see beauty in the broken. Knowing it wants more than anything to be chosen. Being a beast for the chosen... For the beauty of the beast of the chosen is so affectionate when appreciated, that's the respect it gets. I see beauty in the broken. They know exactly what to do with the chosen.

I Think I Might

I could smell the sweetness as I entered that cinna
bun.
Her honey glazed my erection like a candy coated
Chevy.
My mind drifts constantly wondering about the
stability of her levy.
Sea level is way below and it's amazing how deep I
go...
The "P" has the power and it's no point in fighting.
"Imma *pimp*," is what I tell myself so falling is the
last thing I'm inviting.
Geez she's a keeper...
Two years in and no thought of being a creeper. Is
it my maturity or the fact that she comforts me?
I really can't see past her leaving me.
I think I need to wife her. You know...
Gucci hand bag, Vera Wang, red bottoms, damn
right, bruh.
Imma fight the negatives ya hear me!
Call it cuffing if you want but imma keep her here,
near me.
Solo be the fool to lose on a good love, ya heard!
I came to realize playing the field is for the birds...
I'm trying build, rest, and bless my life.
Fuck the killing, stealing, and dealing in the middle
of the night.
I need healing, feelings and therapy with
candlelight. Something so soft, I'm hard and ready
to bite!

Rants when she just don't want to do me right.
Teasing me with nookie like, I'm a rookie. Keep
playing, alright?
Have that thang locked up and tied down for the
rest of your life. One baby on the left nip and I'm
on the other one all night.

If By Chance

If there comes a chance to change some of the wrongs into rights, do so appropriately. You find things out as you travel in time. Remembering what you missed in the past. Lessons that became relevant in the present. Wisdom that seemed to be useless until... It's never a bad thing to recognize your faults. It's only bad when you recognize and leave them to fester. Your righteous decision of today will leave a groundwork to deal with in your future, as your poor decisions will, too. Nothing goes unanswered, *EVER*. When you see it, catch it, fix it... Before it gets out of control.

Intro

She came and sat sideways to fit in the booth. The place was crowded, so I figure I was the lucky dude. Didn't know she knew me already. I was a regular and so had she been a little steady. I'm always into my soup... See it as I'm trying to be summa time fine by the summa time this time...

She spoke as I gazed into her eyes. She was fly and I'm a pimpin' type of guy. You know... Kool, mellow, and nice with a conversation. Her mindset was wonderful. She gave me her number and I never called. When she saw me, she started to stall... all the time. So she asked after a month or so what the deal was... I told her I was on a dog mission and just couldn't see having bad blood between us. She agreed and said, "God is amazing." I seconded the motion and said, "Do tell."

She, too, was plotting to sabotage me as well. *Umph this bitch*, is what I'm thinking... why I asked? Her line was, the last time she fell in love at first sight ruined her life... so her mind had been telling her one thing but her heart another. I handed her my number this time. Told her complete her mission if she chooses... Decide which of the two she would listen to.

Imma hard headed mofo. I like to start fights with your mind and heart. Let them conflict feelings until your eyes are open wide. Emotional maintenance, I call it. She loved me at first sight. Just lets me know she's a hopeless romantic like myself. Let's see how we end up, might just be worth the breath.

It Was All

Issa dream, a nightmare, a practical joke of some sort. Imagine being the one and then *BAM*! You're asking for support... Daily deposits 'cause you're needing, feeling, fiending like you've had your last and you're about to crash. Fix it for seconds and now you're a blast, up and glad like you're interested in whatever it was that made you laugh... Issa dream... You never saw such a chilling thing. A nightmare when it's gone, a bad joke when you see the scheme of things... Like, who could've even "done you that?!" How could they "do you something?" Issa emotional high... hurricane of winds and debris and water from sea-to-see you in confusion from... Being the one, now you're not... Issa love-a-thon on the run.

It Matters To Me Not, What You Think

Lord knows what my mind can think of.
As long as the Lord knows, what the rest of society
doesn't understand is their business.
I'm bigger than a box, a circle, a triangle...
Any shape you try to compare me to, I'm already
outside of those parameters.
It's in your best interest to do the same.
Conforming to laws that are unlawful and biased...
I can't believe that the shit they're trying to impose
on me is a rite of passage.
These demons want you to accept nonsense as if it
were common sense. I'm not dumb, common sense
huh...
What I know about that is, if it doesn't feel right...
Then, it isn't right. #SocietysfinestIAM #king #beast
and that feels so good to me.

It's Clear To See

Sitting here reminiscing of "who" had two reasons to...

Buckle down and do what it do. I can remember a time or four, for sure...

But then, the wind blew you, your compassion and love into left field...

Foul ball!

All this for no return phone call at all. Brawl like cats and dogs over love and affection.

Flexing on the gram, as if you've been neglected. When in all actuality...

You've been rejecting (halt) now it gets clearer. You're rejecting the present for that's not what you want near.

How foolish of a heart, a mind I'm in possession of... Fuck that there. Now class is in session of... lesson of, truth and loyalty. Might not have known then but now... I know it's me.

Keep Pushing Baby

Awkward isn't it? Well, it should be. #SocietysfinestIAM and they, could never be me. Try as much as you want to replace and continue to come up short. Life is a lesson and yours will be thoroughly taught. Count your experience as far as us, as a blessing. Now you will always know, what the best is. The rest will have a standard that's hard to meet. The same patience I gave you, you have to give thee. The time will come when you will meet, someone either close or better than me... Lmao or maybe not. Either way still... you had a spot so, keep on.

Keisha

I need a gangsta chick like Keisha, from New Jack
City.
Screaming "Rock-a-Bye Baby" as I suck on her titty.
I need a sexy chick like Keisha, you know, the one
from Belly.
Give it to me like she would, ass shaking like jelly.
A chick like Keisha, she sang so good... Cole, cold
world, I know she'd treat me good.
Give me a Keisha like refa, a chick so hye...
Society's finest, with her I'll fly.
I like a Keisha who's mine, down to ride that bike.
#SocietysfinestIAM #king #beast she loves to
stroke that pipe... I need a Keisha.

Know Your Surroundings

If it doesn't look like chicken, don't expect it to
taste like chicken...
Assuming something with no concrete evidence...
Is just risky.
So when things present themselves as what they
are, don't try to alternate the view to make
yourself comfortable.
You needed to know and now you do.
Chicken...truth...only comes in one form...
Real.
I don't care how many ways you prepare it, it's still
the same ol' chicken.
Know your surroundings.

L's & W's

Kids don't even realize the type of L's parents take
just so they can have a W!!!
Some loved ones don't even realize, the back
burner you put your shit on while theirs is on the
front eye heating up and taking off!!!
Even friends or lovers...
Can't even fathom the real depth of loyalty,
devotion and honesty...
You have given someone (them) non-blood but
treated equally as if we came from the same
womb!
That's love! What has to be learned needs to be
taught ASAP!
The pages turn whether you can read or not,
whether you're on the speed or same page as the
average crowd or over achievers or not!
Yet people demand and abuse what's chosen to be
given.
Tisk tisk... Risk this...
We all are guilty of the bullshit! We need to stop it.

Legally Stoned

National 4/20 plenty... gas and ass, higher than a
cloud gimme,
Mo' of the dro, loud screams, and moon rock. Cock
that ass up, slow motion, boom, pop...
A cloud of smoke and choke on this philly.
Chocolate flavored stogie, don't hold me just let
me split it.
Lick and fill it up with meeee...
Lemme light it. Damn that ass phat, puff and pass,
are you excited?
Stroke with every exhale, I'm getting hye.
I see "you" getting hye, too, don't lie.
The best beat in the world to some geek shit...
Weed is my pussy, 4/20 I needs it.

Like A Thief In the Night

Handcuffs and baby oil, California king bed and
satin sheets.
This is the way I love to sleep.
Perpetrator silently moving through the house...
I'm not even sleep, yes Lord I'm about to show out!
I have a spot in the floor that always squeaks.
Any moment now, I'm 'bout unleash the beast!
Suddenly, I got nervous. Breathing rapidly...
I saw those big eyes staring at me. So I kept
breathing slowly 'til they got closer. The perp
kneeled down slowly and that's when I pulled them
closer.
Firm grip around the waist, firm grip the perp had
on my private space! That's when I knew it was
going down, seriously...
I slammed them to the bed, viciously. Put one arm
behind the back, then the other. Gave that ass a
smack and then another.
Tussling in the covers...
Man forget them handcuffs, I'm ready to fuck her
ass up.

Living As

Double identity, her maiden name
from her marriage name...

Alter ego, her *Lois Lane* versus her
Superwoman.

That's what a name change is
supposed to mean. Take her from
average to **outstanding**...

The haters wonder why she's
demanded in your life. *YOUR WIFE* is a
mystery to **remain**.

I can't be your *HUSBAND* and you
continue to be lame in the game.
Same dame anybody can hold claims
to.

Bitch please, my last name means life
and prosperity.

You and I, whatever else we gain, ya
see...

These nameless male figures wouldn't
dare take a chance to enhance in
matrimony.

Now, hold up though...

Lois, this ain't that bullshit.

YOUR priors are sealed in the past, no
new convictions if your...

Maiden name is no longer your last.

Lost Ones

She looked at me, something like she knew me. I
was on the train bumping my groovy music.
She said she loved me, at least that's what my
heart felt...
She stared deep into my eyes and I swear she felt
how my heart felt.
I never said anything the entire time, we rode just
looking...
I turned away a few times and felt her eye pushing.
To make sure I wasn't tripping, I moved.
Low and behold her eyes did too.
This is true, what am I to do???
Seriously,
She's more beautiful than a candy apple covered
in nuts.
A pure work of art, I can't make this shit up!
I'm so comfortable with me, just... it's my
situation.
I'm a man above all and I'm particular about dead
end confrontation.
A pet peeve of mine, I don't dine... waste nobody's
time because I'm a stickler about mine!
Gotta get ya shit together and in line. Beauty
comes a dime a dozen but love is rare to find.
Blowing my mind... the signs are all there.
I've been down so long and it just isn't fair.
I know she loves me, I just need to meet her.
She licked her lips flirting like, I need to beat her.

Every inch of ecstasy, damn it's getting hot...
My situation is a mofo, damn it needs to stop.
Gotta get ya shit together.

Love & Respect

Love & Respect: one is no good without the other.
Love for a person will make you want to act a fool
on a person
BUT,
Respect for the person won't let you do it.
If a person can't respect you enough to show some
common courtesy,
Their love isn't coming from the right place.
There is negative and positive love.
There is no such thing as negative or positive
respect...
It's just respect and respect is positive period!
Remember that...
Positive love has positive respect which comes
with positive actions...

Love Changes Things

The love turned left after the right, then led to a dead end. She began playing games as if I was a needy heathen...

Miss me wit' the Cracker Barrel dishes, I'm superb in the kitchen... baby these recipes are why you continue to pull up to the table needing another fixin'.

Let the light shine over the fog. Seeing clear that you've been hurt, so you want to treat me like a dog!

Love, this pimpin' at its greatest...

Don't ever in this lifetime try to debate, shake, or break it.

When my feelings are true... This is the honesty you would do best to pursue!

Otherwise... you get the kaboot. Now go on and choo choo you rooty poot. #SocietysfinestIAM #king #beast. "The curve"

Love Games

She knew my type, knew exactly what I liked,
she crushed and crashed all of that in just one site.
She calculated strategies behind the lines, simply
touched parts of my mind that had not been fucked...
Caressed my neck and cherished my nuts. She
impressed the God in me with much love...
Stuck to the scripts, improvised nothing but the
technique.
She surprised me one day when I brought out her inner
freak... Yet and still we haven't made love properly.
She signed over her property and that's when I rocked
her B. The double cross captured me 'cause that was her
scam.
HOTT DAMN, my heart she locked away. As she walks
away with a twist...
I sit holding my stick *WISHING* she let me hit.
I'm so damn horny!
She gives what is needed and we both be looking all
corny...
To the rest who don't understand, soulmates walk with
no earthly plan.

Mental Mindset Checks

And I said to myself,
"Self"
Motivation is energy,
Energy from vast sources,
Constantly feeding off each energy source it's
connected to so there's no chance of energy ever
being depleted
Therefore
"Self"
If energy is being taken from your source of energy,
That source of energy is not a motivating source for
your energy... Cut that ish off

Mimosas and Us

What kind of drink do you want, love? Mimosas for
breakfast, love making and tequila margaritas for
the interlude?
Following a lunch filled with grilled stick and stiff
stuffed fits that lift calories away like calisthenics,
champagne forever, Kama Sutra forever, raising the
bar as high as your limbs go... never saying never.
Dinner is well deserved, delivered throughout any
type of weather.
#societysfinestiam #king #beast #sho_u_right, best
believe it's going down on multiple levels.
Intoxicating metaphors with passionate actions I'm
getting better...
Acquainted with the emotional lanes that shift
speeds quicker than *The Fast & Furious*.
Purring from your kitten, vibrating like it's very,
very curious.
Honestly thinking, I'm speaking from a place of
sheer curiosity... a monstrosity of emotions inside
of me.
Damaged and on the edge hanging for dear
breath... such a freak for nature talking freaky 'til
death.
Champagne forever, toasting to sex appeal and
hours of appealing sex forever.
Never too much, never too much, never too much
Gimme those orgasms, moans, scratches and
continue to spread and give it up!

Say whaaaat?
Your mind has never been touched in this manner
before?
Could it be, me... or the stroke of the clock for
which we meet?
Or both at the same time, just preparing us both
so we could respect...
The best that life has to offer. What do you want to
drink, love?
Champagne forever, I gotta full bottle.

My Baby's Father

My baby daddy is da truth! That statement is living... Friends and family being nosey about your feelings. Ya girlfriends saying, "Damn boo, you getting thick!" As you reply, "I know girl, I'm gettin' DICK!"

My baby daddy is da truth! Ten times Golden Corral... Buffet is crazy you have to sit back and laugh... He got missionary Monday, from the back Tuesday, ride him so wild Wednesday I can barely move, slurp him down Thursday, swallow it all Friday, whatever u want Saturday, and making love Sunday.

My baby daddy is da truth! He got me getting jealous. I know those his sisters but those heifers love telling... If I had it my way, he wouldn't talk unless summoned. The way he whispers the shit he whispers, keeps me cummin'. I know I ain't the only. I know that it had to be others... So I work his ass out so there won't ever be another.

My baby daddy is da truth! He ALWAYS keeps it real with me. Even when he wrong he finds a way to win against the enemy... Even if I'm wrong he takes his time, being a friend to me.

My baby daddy is da truth and I got to overstand it... These are the things #SocietysfinestIAM has the upper hand with. She told me her baby daddy is da truth.

New Definition

Ask if you must do so, remember the answers to
questions you do know...
Confirmation is just due though. Can't you handle
not getting exactly what you're due?
So, only if your heart can take that beat, only if
your mind can miss some sleep...
Only if that breath won't be missed. To actually
hear it in existence, will be your own infliction...
Your own thrust for the lust of being hurt... but
that's love for your ass!!!
Like knowing white holds dirt, smoke comes from
fire, and life is filled with death.
Diamonds are truly precious but... it's before the
cuts that determine its depth.
Heal your emotion with your own truth, no matter
what you're told.
The belief is in you, the proof. A lie can turn your
life into a dream...
You have to know the difference and what the
meaning truly means.
So don't hide from the fact and don't invite
opinion... #SocietysfinestIAM giving you a new
definition!!

No Lie

No lie, the simplest way to describe how I'm seeing
our future is like this...
You
Two pieces of bread.
Me
The meat in between the bread! 👀
Then once we get to...🖐 And...👋Then...💥 Boom!
Here cums the sauce, salt, pepper, cheese, extra
meat 'cause you greedy.
Late night 'cause you needy. Appetite increases,
'cause the metabolism is speeding. Burning off the
calories with every deep skeeting.
Revitalized energy with every deep beating...
Caressing the inner with heavy deep breathing.
Repeating as prescribed for intense connect-ing.
Keeping the bodies intertwined clearly
respect-ing...
The power of the passion in good lov-ing. Enough
to know it's healthy when it's frequent and it helps
to cut down on all the fussing...
Make a sandwich as often as you can and don't
forget nutting!!!

Not Even You!

I so love the ride, the glide back and forth in
between your thighs.
The look in your eyes as you cried... trying your
damnedest to hide behind your pride,
but I took that.
Respect this, it's not even you, it's your neglected,
reflected, emotion that...
I cast a spell of pleasurable experience as you
battle with the motion of the currents.
Not being in control and trying to run from it but
I...
Own your body in which
I,
Stroke your soul as
I,
Brainwash your mind then
I,
Hear you claim it's mine... so
I,
Intertwined your spine... it's not even you, it's
what you pursue.
All of your dreams,
I see me in them...
Your fears are all of me.
Tears of infinity...
Finna be, your homie lover friend and your worst
enemy.
The world you desire revolves around me! My
energy, powers your generators, mad 'cause my
nature been a player. It's not even you... it's the

abuse. Knowing that I do love you. You love me...
Not like I love you. You still pleased the beast. But...
it not even you. It's me.

Nothing To Lose

Let me be it... your daddy, your best friend, your
pimp.
Can u see it?
The guidance that I will fulfill. Direction, pleasant
thoughts, satisfaction.
Distraction from the bullshit when you need some
action... one phone call away, there it awaits.
Regularly I provide above average ... food, water,
and compliments you gotta have it.
The lady knows not but has the info to be
informed.
The gentleman has the doctrine documented
solidified in its history.
The heritage has always left mysteries to figure out
in the sight of plain...
Being in good observation it's your duty to
completely obtain,
With a stain or two because it tends to get messy.
Pressure like a mofo
BUT,
It's the way you learn so come bless me. With your
presence and devotion and affection.
Let me, be your daddy, your best friend, your pimp,
your direction.

Another Episode

She was featured on an episode of "The First 48,"
charged her with killing emotions on the first date.
"60 Minutes" interviewed her and asked,
"What were your motives?"...
She said, "I have the right to remain silent because the
cases are still open."
Poking for some justice when I met her.
I became her alibi and I, just wouldn't let her... kill me.
Shit got so serious, it became a serial matter. She would
literally smash all of the material data...
No evidence, no finger prints, no DNA.
She swallowed every fragment that would, skeet her
way.
She made a clean escape with no trace...
The Feds had been on her tail, waiting at her place.
Called me her accomplice her pimp tried to put me in her
space.
Macking is a freelance job, fuck out my face.
#societysfinestiam, to be continued at a later date...

Package Delivery

Lemme get an I.O.U. in the
A.T.L.

Mail it to M.I.A. special
delivery.

Unwrap it with express
feelings.

Redeem it at the nearest open
room with an open bar.

Show proof of validation. Yes,
ownership is very necessary as
you turn regular into
legendary.

Nights into afternoon
checkouts. Hondas into
Rovers...
Rolling over, touching and
grabbing, pulling closer... to
your dreams.

#SocietysfinestIAM providing everything.

Pieces Of A Painted Picture

She painted a picture so believable. All I wanted to do was, "believe in you."

Put your troubles on my back and proceed with you... changing your perception of what that nigga instilled in you.

Captain Save-a-Heart, a mind so you would be my "hoe," my "bitch."

My moment felt properly handled by the emotional maintenance of the way love flows.

Truth of the matter, it was never my battle. The war was much bigger than I could have ever imagined.

The picture was so faded and distorted from plain view. She painted so clearly through words like "how much I NEED you."

Which was true... but you ain't "WANT" me.

There lays the difference in the plot. I'd rather want it than need it. Simply in the way that it's treated... believe me cuz.

Prescription Filled

I sent my folks a Rx for some dick. Pick it
up at the "W" room 69, it's thick...
Guaranteed to cure that sickness called
(bitch) u been tripping a lil' bit. The
question had been arising about why the
hotel is known well...

The bell hop said the guest in 69 fuck so
hard all the letters fell and all that was left
was the "W". It was fixed it a time or two
but it made no use because when we fell
through, well, they came to know what
we came to do.

The manager said the way they screw, it's
a "W"hirlwind for two, just leave the "W"
until they're through. Regarding the
position of the rest of the letters... Ahh
the hell with it,
these mofo ain't going to never let up.

Place Your Bets

I bet you can't just make love and exit... Not to me. 'Cause see, imma take a piece of your everything. When your phone rang... your ringtones gonna change. If it ain't me, it's gonna be Plain Jane. Decline and voicemail for everythang. After we... nothing else, will ever feel the same. Even a simple bath... You'd rather wait or if it came to it... You would take the risk and stank. Cause with we, it's more guaranteed than the bank. What I'm simply saying is, you wouldn't function or even want to thank... And it's mutual, that's why we tighter than a chain... Closer than the bricks of a house. Stronger than the jaws of an alligator snapping and they can't figure it out. Wondering how the love lasts. Have we ever experienced a drought? Through it all, we vowed to always talk it out.

Put That On Everything

Beat my meat then skeet, skeet, skeet... Damn baby, let me just eat, eat, eat. You can tell I have a healthy appetite for the passion. I won't back away from this plate. As scrumptious as you're looking, seconds are not up for debate. Obviously, it gets deep as I dive between your thighs. Surprised, I think I could just cry. I'm truly amazed, baby... I need you as my main lady. I just like to love nasty... Ask me and it shall be done. Let my mind run and you just won't know what's to become! Pleasure to please you, miss. *Umph*, I see you've been anxious to kiss... The lips of a real lover. Hiding nothing but my pride inside your shell. If you're interested then come figure me well. It's not too complicated at all. Communicate, be honest, and keep these (balls) hanging from the window to the walls, as you should already know because it's common sense. Be that slut who's worth all the expense. You know, the one the rest wish they could be... The one who keeps satisfaction on point, evidently. She deserves a ring. Just me and you, I put that on everything.

Real Spit

You're scared to prosper, take a chance,
fall not "fail"
learn and revise to better your life, doesn't mean
someone else is supposed to not achieve their
goals in life...
just because someone excels in a sense that
learning improves the quality over quantity doesn't
mean you have the right to
purposely,
sabotage their gains because you're so short
coming into your own.
That's the quickest way to lose overall, when you
refuse to congratulate success whether it's minimal
or major. Get your shit str8 or sit back and watch
someone else as they get their shit together.

Respect Is A Must Fool

I was always led to believe that ultimately there is a sense of pride and a fondness for the one you're committed to...

The one you're in love with, that someone who makes you proud to call them your one and only.

Nothing is perfect... true,

BUT!

Nothing short of being grateful that, that someone is always your best qualified whatever... that's more than a goal...

It's a part of a good night's sleep. Honestly that's "deep."

Who's in your bed??? "Joy or pain," "Pride or shame?"

Satisfaction Is A Must Fool

Ain't no propaganda behind it...

Satisfaction is a must.

Trust, that's the agenda for anyone of us. Thrust...

Rush, through traffic. Extra sauce on the wings, more conversations in between this, that, and the third.

Choosing the "most" appropriate seductive nouns and verbs. Choice of words to guarantee to get you there...

Satisfaction.

Believe that... it's a must too. No one does what they do knowing that pleasure ain't got time to play.

Listen to what I say...

I don't advocate breaks or other dealers for the cake or nothing of the sort.

HOWEVER, you never settle down for less, clown. Everybody deserves what they put out to be given back round for round, beats by the pound.

Alls I'm trying to convey is...

No matter how you play, stimulating each other's focal point is the only way.

Satisfaction is a must foo...

Sexy Is As, Sexy Does

Imma fan of everything sexy, classic at heart. Voluptuous, yes, and dangerous by far...

When it comes to her smarts, she can crank up a lecture. Turn around and bow down the illest intellectual.

Sexual so special, couldn't even get next to. Choosing on a pedestal, members only respectable.

Nothing out of the ordinary, hereditary a visionary.

Heritage exceeds her, so future she carries a seed, bruh.

Dedicated to succeeding her... Motivation is light speed the... Future of it all, she stepped up to overachieve.

Make you a true believer, nourishes the soul she feeds a... Helping hand of the plan and MAN, this is what we need, *duh*!

Sexy imma fan of, stand strong and in demand of that queen imma man for and best believe imma stand for...HER.

She & I

She knew my habits; she knew I was an addict.

She knew, soon as I came home from work, I had
to have it...

She knew I was fixated on the bunny rabbit. She
hopped, skipped, and jumped on it just for daddy.

Like a pressure cooker sealing the meal... She was
a hot piece of pussy for the kill.

She never ever let me down, I'm talking for real.

When the feelings are mutual, you know its trill...

I could do just about what I wanted.

Lady was a classy, jazzy kind of woman. Had a side
to her, in her performance that would make you
feel anointed.

The gods had to specifically craft her for one
special...

Talking 'bout nothing could break her professional,
until I...

Whip it out and put her on the pedestal. Lady
asked, was I...

extra-terrestrial?

Out of this galaxy loving my level of deep
intellectual feedback.

#SocietysfinestIAM she and I are the same.

She Deserves Greatness

She sits awaiting your arrival, just to
depart once you've arrived.
Jive to the cause, you pause awaiting
an applause.
How rude dude?
Your performance hasn't even
began...
Again, that's the cloudy head we're
working with, yet the woman
continues to boast in hopes of
forever...
Never to think about uplifting her ego
enough...
Thanks to a million prospects, your
project has "failure" up to come...
#SocietysfinestIAM number 1!

Shows Up to Show Out

She takes her time when it's regular, but I tell you
she's a beast when she's on another level.
Pedals her mountain bike like a cross country race.
Adrenaline rushing as she wipes the sweat off her
face...
Taste the victory, baby knows she's gonna
win.
It's like she's the only one racing, nobody's gaining
on her, Fin.
Umph...umph...umph,
so exciting looking at her with the wind justa
blowing thru her hair,
I'm getting the best of this. Oh my, it seems like I
can't control her erotic behavior.
I tried to tell her days ago that it was time, but she
ignored my advancements,
now she's gonna pay for it.
Slave for it... She was made for it.
She ran outta breath, so I helped her savor it.
Laid her on her stomach and gave her "it." She
"came" cross the finish line and yes,
yes, she earned the title.
Tour de love and these miles she's rode, she's my
American Idol.

Short Story Review

The scene was thicker than Heinz smothered over a juicy Angus burger str8 off the grill. Baby girl who'd been choosing all night was two times thicker, you hear me! I heard about her from a young cuz on the block... Said she was a hard deal to play. No lie, I know who I am and all, but it made me wonder why she choosing so hard, you know? I figured she saw me a time or two and seemed to like how I moved in the hood. Who knows? But, I sure wasn't gonna let it pass me by. I also wasn't going to pursue it either. At least not first! Imma muhfuckin' pimp, that's not what I do.

I stepped in the direction where lil' lady was posted up, just to bait the fish or what have you. And yeah, I buy a drink and offer it to her. She accepted and turned around and paid for me one as well. No problems with that. I asked her name and she said whatever you wanna call me is fine... So I told her I don't do names so she needs to answer to whatever comes out my mouth. Eyes wide she laughed and said, "Ok daddy." She never asked me mine for two reasons I suppose, she already knew it or what she's heard it was and/or the no name protocol was in affect for me as well. Any rate, it is what it is... I don't trust her or me for that matter...

Two weeks went by and ol' gurl and I had been kicking it kool and mellow. A couple of dates, sexting and talking like we had been lovers for years, split up and catching back up on old times and what not. I hadden smashed her and neither had she offered. I could see that impressed lil' mama a lot... For me I was really just trying to find her angle. I noticed that I remembered seeing her a time or two outside of the neighborhood and just didn't know that was her. She well-known... I got her name just by describing her to my 'round da way patnas. Nobody seems to have nothing on this chick other than she play hardball. "Y'all can kick it, smoke, drink, whatever, but you ain't diggin' in her draws at all." Is this her hustle 'til whoever gets tired and drops her?

I got tired of thinking and decided to shake sum. So one night I told her what I wanted and she agreed. Simple as that. No date, no food, no drinks... Just me and her at a Marriott outside of town. Just in case this was a set up. She didn't know we were heading out of town and funny 'cause she didn't even care. She let loose as soon as she saw we were outside city limits. Sucked me off on the highway, two, three times... The strange thing, the whole drive we hadden said six words. Maybe it was just anticipated gestures that did the talkin'...

Once we got about 2 hours out, we pulled up to the room. Checked in and got str8 to it... After about the 3rd or 4th round is when it seemed like the ice really had been broken and we began talking like we usually would have. That's when the confessions came out. I knew something was up, I just couldn't put a finger on it. I asked why she was lurking the way she was and why when I said what I said she was all in and why she went all around the world wit dez other niggas just to get to me??? "Homework," she said... All them other niggas was just helping her wit her homework on me. Said half of the cats were hoes and the other half were bitches. Pretty much said she knew I was a clean cat wit a past and that's what she wanted. She knew I had plugs and just wanted to know how deep shit really was. Them niggas can't hold water. She said you would have thought she was the Feds the way they run their mouths when they get comfy wit a bitch. I couldn't do nuttin' but laugh 'cause the truth is what it is.

She was trying to see if I had a woman, kids, the house 'n picket fence set up. Then she hit me with the bomb... #tobecontinued....

Situationship

She came at an expensive price. I laid down with
her on that faithful night.

Time and time again we chose it, knowing it was
nothing strong enough to hold it

I just didn't care and she just couldn't help herself.
I loved her gratitude and she loved that I was
always there.

I learned her ways and if they weren't...

She made them her ways for the moment.

Her little getaway from what was coming. Things
that were present way before me.

Things that were too much to focus on and along
came we.

Along came pleasure, satisfaction and she, made
little noises in between the weeps.

The best of all I had,

she could have been just giving me whatever.

Four off and on years and back and forth and stop.

Last I heard from the woman, she begged for me
to stop.

Through a telephone call and I hadn't said a word.

I think she needed me to save her and was just
afraid that I would.

Sk8 Life

The baddest on 8 wheels...
(She is)
rolling like a big rig Mack truck!!! Glide so smooth,
back, back, back it up.
That's that control that turns me on. Sk8 life...
any song can be a rhythm, any rhythm can be your
move.
Your next move is your best move... betta make
sure it's nice.
The gurlies love a lover on wheels that deals like a,
thief... in the night.
That's right, I've slid up on a corner myself and had
to do
NOTHING but...
handle myself and sure as gold is solid. The sk8 life
had two newly met humans holding hands like two
lovers in college.
See! The first steps in everlasting romance...
sk8 life, mo' game than any pimp and any WO-
MAN.

So Much In Common

When I told her who I was, she immediately asked
what was my sign. I told her #Scorpio... she started
smiling outta her mind. She says, "My first love was
a Scorpio. You're one hell of a man... You can be
sneaky, but you take care of your woman. I'm very
loyal, once a playa chooses, I dun chose. It's mostly
about how far you want to go."
So, I asked her, could I be her second love. Her eyes
fluttered like that's exactly what she'd been
thinking of. She let me know she was staying with
someone. I respected her position and said I
couldn't be that one. She continued the
conversation for like 45 mins... steady giggling and
smiling, as if she was out here fishing. Asking me
where about I was from... I promise like she was
trying to see how she can make something fun.
So, she says, I can talk to you for hours. If it's meant
to be, I will see you sooner than tomorrow. Shook
my hand and politely asked what my name was.
Then she told me hers... like she regretted where
she stayed. Like she wanted me just to come
swoop her away. My, my, dangerous Scorpio when
I play.

Something to Be Proud Of

Show me something worth wanting. Stroking my
ego is okay, but, honestly...

I can get that any day of the week. Peep the
scene... She said to me as I walked to the counter,

"I've seen you somewhere before, some other
encounter a while ago though.

Yeah, yeah, you my friend's brother's homie."

"Maybe," I said and paid for my shit and stepped
off. She was getting off literally, physically, and
mentally. Feeling me, I suppose...

Walked out of the store and she hollered,
"Helloooo!"

I said, "Yoooo!"

I thought, what the hell, let me see what turns
freaks into nymphomaniacs. I attacked her hard, I
see it kind of made her response different.

I really don't know what she thought at that time,
but I tell you one thing, she confirmed she was still
interested.

She blessed me with a hell of a hug and we parted
ways.

It's only been a couple days and regardless of what
you say, what she's doing is waayyyy more
interesting.

So, show me why I should continue to be your
blessing. Imma man above all and baby doll, I'm
the cream of the crop, flaws and all.

I'm not even trying to be petty by telling you about another woman. You just act as if I can't get another woman.

Huh...

what's that you're mumbling. Oh, that's your stomach...

Funny how you're hungry as I'm always getting to the money. Stopping my show like a monkey in distress.

LMAO!

Woman you're a mess. Caught up in your dress, I lost a bit of sense... That's part of the process, a learning experience.

Sometimes, All the Time

Feeling the pain of your body and the neglect of my own.
Spending sleepless nights Instagramming on a phone.
Paths crossed and DMs lost, relatively small to have had paid a big cost.
Everyone needs attention...
everybody wants love.
Someone wants you...
somebody doesn't want you enough.
Despite the self-esteem other people feel is over the top. The confidence that's boiling hot out the pot...
The recognition seen in your face, walk, talk, and personality. Despite all that shines, there's still some type of discrepancy.
Something just ain't right!
As the sunrise hits your eyes and you bid your tired soul another sleepless night. Sometimes are worse than others. Other sometimes aren't even noticed.
It seems like a long road ahead
but...
you just have to stay focused.

Stallion Status

Stallion status!!!

She can have it. Grab it and ride like she's a master at it.

A habit of hers,

LOVE to explore the structure of the mechanism. Inspection of the mechanics...

The dynamic of the performance. Owning such a thorough breed increases her stimulation when intimacy drives her anticipation...

Stallion status is her destination.

See her on her high horse and watch her blossom, her glow shines brighter than a sun ray...

She sparkles like a moon lit night. Stars gaze over candlelight and you.

Stallion through and through.

Private Kentucky derbies are held. Suit up and ride and stride as she yells...

Giddy up!!! Yes!!! Giddy up!!

What a breath of fresh air it is for the woman.

After a long day's work...

It's this moment she longs for... Give her what it's worth. #stallionstatus

Stay Woke

You couldn't ask for something greater. Cater to
your ego, making you feel greater.

That's the circle of love. Feeding each other.
Constantly giving one the proper nutrition to rev
their engine.

Definition, volume, and mass appeal,

but to whom...

Outsiders envy like the elephant in the room. It's
noticeable from a mile away...

Whereas the foul come in to play, trying to
damage a family. They can't stand it...

Temptations are very sexy to the eye. Underneath
though...

Where does the truth lie?

Try, try, and try to see with your inner over your
outer. Pleasure of five minutes or so with a lifetime
of doubters...

Or ecstasy in a lifetime with a doubt of... who's
true to you?

Chop and screw sex suckas and continue to
pursue... happiness above all. Pay attention to the
fake love that's involved to see you fall.

Stay woke.

Taking the Initiative

I kissed her once and it began a fight. She said I had
some nerve. It wasn't even our first date.

I replied,

"The kiss is what will let me know if it was even
worth a date from the get-go." That was ten years
ago.

Three break-ups and two kids. I admit, the break-
ups are how the kids got here...

You know, break-up... To make up... That's all, we
do.

I've asked her twice just to be clear that I wanted
her hand. She accepted as usual.

But what is it that turns happily ever after into, wtf
did we do?

I've cheated,

only because I was misled by false emotions.

She says she never did... But has been caught in
lies that would send your ass up the road for life!

Yet that unhealthy, live wire love connection won't
fade.

That one hurdle in the race that just keeps
knocking you down with every attempt to jump.

Any who, going through it without flaws is priceless and these days ain't shit cheap...

Including joy and/or pain.

With open minds to the next chapter, the phone rings ten minutes after.

As you would think it was a congratulations on the opposite end... Fucking shittin' me...

Nothing but more hoorah and you wouldn't believe from who this time...

The Blessings of True Beauty

Beauty is a gift, a blessing... not all pretty people are beautiful. Actually, it's no such thing as an ugly person, just an ugly soul... spirit or mindset. Beauty has stages. Ultimate beauty is a platform that's won, not given. It's earned, through beautiful acts done on a humbled stage in front of millions or simply just one witness... yourself. It's not for recognition. Just a mere gesture of love that's wanting to spread itself. So, when you have the looks that go with the action... you are the one who's blessed. So be thankful and pay it forward.

Therapeutically Better

I'm hands down one with the therapy of mind
stimulation, no one can administer conversation
like I do...
As well as energetic, I respect all emotions and
attend to each emotional experience individually...
i.e. emotional maintenance...
Lastly, as a man of my caliber... I see beauty for
way more than how beautiful you are,
but more so as how beautiful you will become.
Beauty never ages, only rejuvenates as beauty
gets wiser.

There Was And Now There Is Not

This, that, and the third weather. You should have
jumped on it when you were being chosen, but you
didn't so now, as hot as it is...
You the one frozen 'cause the conditions aren't in your
favor, so a major player pulled out the Now and Laters
in multiple flavors.
The reserve stash 'cause, at the time it was about
something that would last, and you passed up the
winning pick...
See the team winning trick.
Wanna, "Hey stranger, let a kitty get a lick of the
winning stick."
Oh really, you don't say. #SocietysfinestIAM and I don't
play...
the radio stations. I'm satellite waving. Branding babies
into their rightful places. Faces hate it in their
demonstrations.
Baby look...
there are many places but here just ain't one of them.
It's a cold winter ahead and an even hotter summer.
Your decision your karma. As she walks away, she says...
"What a bummer."

Thinking Of Change

I was laughing, kicking back and you crossed my thoughts... It's been a fairly short time but still long enough to be an issue.
I was only hoping that you are feeling some type of way as I am. Now damn, don't make this harder than it has to be...
I miss you, I do but...
There's still some G up in me! If I'm outta line, hang up and the picture will be clear.
Again, I'm not talking by myself... Seems like you're still here. I can tell your ear is pressed against the phone firmly.
Is it my voice that lingers now your yearn starts to burn deep?
The times, the times were too fast to even decipher good, bad, or ugly.
I just know good was felt and how ugly it's been since you left. Whether you care or not is what's boggling my mental...
We did a lot of stuff and that part is what I'm trying to find sentimental.
Was it lust and no kind of fundamentals... No structure upon the emotions just reckless rolling??
In questioning our actions, activities, and accomplishments during this time frame. Our long- and short-term goals were never there...
Ahhh, just forget it!

You made it obvious that shit was awkward and not
how you saw living your life.
Now I've sparked a flame, is that why you have a
tear in your eye??
If I would've known this call would've brought you
here, I would've freshened up, gotten you a beer.
Come here baby, I never meant to push you away...
Us as men sometimes don't know how to say stay.
I know your life is a book on a day-by-day journey...
So, I just want to narrate the rest by making you a
wife, my sweet honey.

Thoughts Of the Mind

I haven't said much lately, there's so much going on
in America that to capitalize on every event is
impossible...
in a timely manner that is.
But I say this from the deepest respect for life in
general.
It's crazy how life begins as a beautiful baby comes
in and you must tend, fend, and nurture this life as
it grows into its own.
Death comes through its daily perspective and
takes whomever's time has come whether too
soon or late. Nobody has a genuine respect for life
like we used to have.
It's gotten too normal to kill and move on to the
next thing. I'm no saint, no sensitive Sally or
nothing of that nature...
but I DO HAVE A BIGGER RANGE for the morality of
life. Senseless violence will never be acceptable.
Real gangsters don't want problems from other
real gangsters, that's a fact.
There is no love for each other. You don't have to
like me
BUT AT LEAST LOVE MY LIFE AS IF IT WAS YOUR
LIFE. Then and only then will compassion come into
play. Thoughts of doing the next man shady just to
gain a few cents is irate and irrational. Think about
it and you decide.

Time After

Time after time, rhyme after rhyme, line after line.
All I see is fine after fine, dime after dime, shine
after shine.
Wondering is it mine after mine, being blind after
blind just trying...
To see the light.
I ain't lying after love, love is lying after me... The
hassle of the tree came with planting the seed.
Potting the right soil... Finding the right oil.
Digging the right hole... Solidifying the right mold.
Baby steps before the big leap. Counting sheep
trying to get to sleep.
Aiming to always please. Even if it's the pleasure I
never see.
Circumstantial above facts. Propaganda in all acts.
That 97 Love Jones in 95! Way before my time, way
before my grind...
I'm!
Just a youngin' with a grown-up mind. An old soul
with a heart that's primed...
Like that old jalopy that just won't give up trying.
Every time you turn the key it cranks even if it ends
up dying.
Turn it again!
Fire up *growl*!
'Cause the motor is fine. It's the upkeep that falls
short and...
Well, over time, it dehydrates from lack of
stimulation, no TLC from all that driving.

Time to trade it in and invest in the worthy, the
stable. Old-school models are fossils, just ain't able.
Coupe it out in a foreign, I suppose it's able...
To keep up with speed being it's new to the table.
To be continued...

Time vs. Feelings

Times like this is when the weather is just so cold
and relaxing, brings memories of when I had you all
warmed up climaxing...

Nice ass room with mirrors on the wall. Watching
the playback action calling audibles and all.

At the time it was like two inches of snow. A
perfect situationship for nobody to know.

Any and everything to do. It was just me and you...
I could have just married you in my mind, thinking
about the feelings we brew...

I'm missing you, yeah so in my emotions right now.
There may be another lover but not like you and I
just figured it out.

Just anywhere, anytime... Sometimes that's the
best way to ease the mind. I really don't know but
you will always be mine.

Tomorrow Maybe

She passes by me daily, I'm sitting all alone. It's about the same time frequency, she's always on her phone.

She nods, her eyes locking, she smiles to cover her disguise; she looks back teary eyed just begging for me to socialize.

But I'm nervous...

My heart has been broken before. I don't want to misinterpret what it is, I won't to treat her like a whore.

Maybe that's what she wants, yet I'm so so confused...

Maybe if she started the conversation then I'd know what to do.

Has she heard about me? I mean, I'm plugged in well. Guess I'll see her tomorrow, guess one way that day will finally tell.

Torn

Torn between what you love and what you want is conflicting. Damaging your own heart between two positions. Deciding on what you love but it isn't what you want...

So, going for what you want but it isn't what you love. Confusion, why it is so hard to decide? The divide that comes along is ripping you up inside. Its pride for what you love and ego for what you want.

It's the choices you made in life that complicates each one. Last year's decision won't have its true view until 10, 12 years in the future.

Immediate are some responses but prolonged are the truth juices. As bitter or sweet as they maybe, who knows? The right or wrong. A, B, or C it goes... deeper than raw sugar dissolving quicker in warm Kool-Aid versus cold. Choosing what's right isn't just about you.

Treat Me Better Than

Even if yeen know, lying is a form of abuse. The neglect to inform someone of the truth endangers a person's wellbeing, their mental status, and their right to be fully aware of what the possibility could be.
It's abuse...
You are at the top of the pole... First come the lies, then the feeling of trying to be in control. It's only a matter of time before your physical activity aggressively unfolds.
Now it's a whirlwind of, verbal words that tear down the soul... I'm here to say that abuse is abuse, man or woman, abuse is cold...blooded.
A hell of a drug...
'Cause abuse gets addictive when you've been brought up in an abusive household. The simplest forms of abuse get so bold... "You say well I ain't whooping their ass."
I just talk kinda fucked up. They push my buttons and now I'm turnt up.
Abuse is abuse,
abuse is cold... blooded.
It can be love, a friendship, work-related, slavery for no compensation. Yeah you might get the overtime but...
It's the way they say... "It's okay." Its "abuse" spills over into regularly scheduled programming. Thinking, *I'd be damned if I let a mofo treat me like a hoe...*

So, again either man or woman just goes for what they know.

Abuse, is abuse...

Abuse is, cold... blooded.

Flooded the mind, heart, and emotional frequencies... mofos get heated 'cause of the abusive tendency. Oh shit, is that a pistol B?

Pop, pop, pop... shouldn't have been, fucking with me.

See I loved, I cared about everything I gave attention to.

Now it's all fucked up because a lie started the interview.

Do you love me?

(Yes)

Do you trust me?

(Yes)

So, who is he?

(Just)

Another reason to abuse your heart, I guess. Abuse is, cold... blooded.

Unappreciated Love

Memoirs of the Unappreciated: street figures get the love, admiration, respect and loyalty. No matter how many hoes ride the coattail, she stays humble and obedient ready to be his everything at the last call. As soon as he realizes that the streets are a dead end and begins to transition into a law-abiding citizen, shit changes. All that "stop running the street" "what about your family" shit becomes a reality. Everything is fine.

Years have passed and stand up is all this mutha jumper knows. So, stand up is how this mutha jumper flows. A few pit falls here and there. Mostly because of her inappropriate behavior and attitude of not having a care.

Buddy has a million ties and a hustle that's impeccable. So shit is kosher for the most part. Ain't it funny how it seems she was down until it's time to be down? The hood is at the door knocking violently. Begging to come in. The hustler plays humble, silencing the turbulent winds. It's a life change he appreciates for the truth of... Being taught that when its time, its time despite what the streets buzz.

All it is, is applying the same mentality to another aspect of the game... But lil' lady don't understand and doesn't appreciate the mechanism there is to obtain. It's a shame other women see and notice a G stays one in the same. Feeble minded women just won't comprehend the relevance.

Unappreciated and fed up... Decision to wise up and change position. Missing the realness of an authentic misses. Add to the value of the king and elevate the pension... Money, wealth, and power only last as long as the intellectual structure remains intelligent. Balance the stick and progress in a unified element.

Appreciate the stability of... Grow out of the past and professionalism for the future. Seasons will change and only the suitable will produce a destination in life with life as its narrator. Hustle through the nonsense and the nonsense will do its own detriment. Memoirs of the unappreciated brotha and the signs are evident.

Understanding the Cause

The champion you are is proven by your success!

The power in your prayers believes you will be blessed. Devote a conscious mind to be a humble servant.

Every testament is a trial,

YOURS will serve its purpose. As impossible as it may seem, you MUST refuse to lose!

Your destination isn't final. NO retreat, NO surrender!

Your next move is your best move, YOU ARE THE NUMBER 1 CONTENDER....

Fifth & End Of the Lift

If you can't be "honest" with me,
"please" don't expect me to be "righteous"
 with you...
#SocietysfinestIAM not even that type of fool.

Wants Are Needs, Too

Wanting to be touched, held and manipulated
vigorously until their time has come to release into
the atmosphere.

Sounds like a winner, wouldn't you say? It's like
second nature, ya know? No real effort needed. All
fun and games, stimulating bits and pieces.

Commercial television and sitcoms are quickly
deleted, just a soundtrack to drown out the, "Come
on baby beat it." "Baby, yes I need it." "Baby yes
it's yours because, damn baby you the deepest."

Treat it like the last and cherish every first time.
Everyone's wanting the best and that you have.

Lucky is a metaphor, while blessed is the truth.
Taking pictures in the booth to commemorate the
life we're going through.
Forever I shall be the protector of the
"P"...

Purity, precious, and pretty damn good nookie!
Lookie lookie, suga. Sweeten my coffee...

Creamer all over the rim, goodness, good googley
moogley couldn't find them... so I, search high and
low.

Not caring how far I had to go. #SocietysfinestIAM #king #beast #sho_u_right Best believe it's going down tonight...

Way Down In the Jungle Deep

The Amazonian river runs so deep. Width and
depth, curves so chic. Blush from a touch of
this big body of water. Chills the hottest temps
down, raises any testosterone beyond the natural
laws of order.
The border of erotic and pornographic addict to
the magic of, natural habitat I just gotta go
swimming. Shimmy shimmy yah shimmy yay.
I like it raw...
Skinny dipping, feeling... that bear claw grip!
Amazonian woman you got that shit...
One sip of your Nile River flowing through...
Wrap me in your vines, so fine flowing down this
river, oh... I set sail on a raft. This Amazonian river
got a lot of ass to grab.

Well Alright

I hope you don't mind me speaking my mind a bit...
I love it when you get explicit, grab the stick. Make
love to it, talking your shit.
Handling the shipment like fragile goods, in the
same token rough housing to check the stability of
the wood.
It's all good,
once the inspector passes it for inspection, time to
take the freight in a different direction.
Protection, knowing you have your license to carry,
murking anything emotionally no physical
technicality.
Practically dominating the sport. Using me as your
stage, your center court.
Up 'n down taking the drill ever so serious. Every
inch as if the measurement has you so curious.
At its purest, the flavor is so succulent on your
taste buds.
Thanking the chef for preparation of the steak
cause, the sauce is so rich, so you say plus...
It's aged perfectly the way you like with no
wait thus, the lust for the bust is a must. The love
you make with the touch of your... "*Excuse me,
what?*"

*Hush, don't discuss, just continue to trust you will
never get enough...*
Well alright.

Well Damn!!!

I go to Starbucks and order a long-haired, thick
redbone.
Cashier asked, "What's that?"
A large caffeinated coffee, 6 sugars, 6 creams...
Damn!
So, then I ordered 2 slim thicks...
Cashier asked again, "What's that?"
2 chocolate chip cookies, damn!!!
Last, I ordered a dozen juicy booty mistresses.
Cashier said, "We out of brain muffins, but we have
Pecky Beckys."
I asked, "What?"
Cashier says, "Cream cheese bagels, damn!!!"

What Do The Lonely?

It gets lonely being the only one who feels the urge
to...
Build up the nerve to,
just to get curved through...
all the prospects that respect the kings being with
queens who patronize the same kings' feelings.
Silence speaks truth already seen in actions.
Actions express death no breath can give life to...
It gets lonely, true.
Being a king who doesn't slay every want-to-be
lady.
Women want to be baby...
Females just want to misplace it...
Gets lonely at the top. For a king without a drop...
Of what most call love is merely just a good fuck.
Love leads to so many other nutts that...
your cup is never empty,
your well never runs dry.
No matter if you're tired...
The passion is lit inside and
it will never die.
Tired and all...
You still fall victim to,
I just want to please which are symptoms of...
Nothing but love.
It gets lonely thinking of...
Love.

What Are Your Plans?

Buried in flurries of snow... Flow of the wind...
Warm cognac shots comfy in the living room end,
tables aside...

Slide in position... Tickle your back, that giggle is
what I've been missing...

Surrounded by theater speaker bumping Sade'...
Cherish this day 'cause taboos fade away. Is this
what they say *one of those getaways to play...?*
Should you remain in place...? As this time withers
away...

Your body gives answers to questions not yet
asked... Just lets me know to continue to finesse
that ass...

Jet lag, mind frame of altitudes of... *ohhh 69 feet*...
As we crawl from up under the sheets dusk begins
to creep...

Dawn is a short journey away... Man, oh man,
what a way to spend an entire day!

A Change In Barometric

When it's 34° at 1 a.m., your natural gas provider
ain't got nothing on them. A lil' rub a dub dub,
snuggle up and what?...

Crack the window a lil' 'cause it's getting heated
up. Thirty-four degrees can bring another seed in
October. The coldest of seasons tends to get a sexy
mofo wrapped up and bent over.
Riding like a Range Rover, through this wilderness
of #beast! #king #Kong what you call it?
The chill still ain't got nothin' on me! Blow that
thang off, on fire I see...
Oh it's 34°, all you really need is me. Increase your
body temperature to, say 69°.
At an angle and dangle your legs... it's the weather
baby, so give me some head.

Let nature change the seasons as nature changes
the physical forms of us... when it's 34°,
it's a must we touch.

When It's Time Nothing Else Matters

I'm at peace with everything except my emotions...
When it's time, it's just time...
There's no negotiation, no bargaining, no
substitute, no way around it.
So many things can interfere with the progress but
that does not eliminate the process.
Like a car that needs oil, it's not just lubricant for
whatever...
It keeps things easy and operating properly...
Nothing dry works fine...
Emotional maintenance for the mind... I'm, at
peace with everything except my emotions.
Who's got the oil to keep my motor rolling?

When The Kitty Calls You First

The phone rang.

I let it go to voicemail. The voicemail was 2 minutes long with a faint cry to it...

I heard the voice pick up bass as it began to say more. More mumbling than speaking...

It was kitty purring, she needed some teaching. Kitty had been bad and disrespectful.

Each one of Kitty's 9 lives were being killed softly... Being sorry don't cut it.

Being loyal does.

When You're Fed Up

And so, it's begun. The beginning of what you
thought you had won. Sucka, keep it real...
That was introductory level
and you failed.
You can't even begin to shadow the levels I've
prevailed. Using as punitive action against yourself,
you should have just learned to increase your
wealth. The net worth needs be worth the net...
It's like you're fishing in a stream with nothing
left... Starving to feed, losing your health.
I've watched and tried to aid but you did it to self.
Meet the demands to redeem a step.
There's work to be done if you want to free
yourself.
On the outside looking in as you plead for help.
Silly rabbits fall for the tricks trying to milk a cow.
The whole while they are going coo-coo for Cocoa
Golden Grahams at my house.

Where Do We Go

Pull it out and let it drip, slide, roll down every inch
from the exit point.
This is to saturate the skin and moisten up the
driest front...
Naturally hydrate and fulfill, give what the body
needs to live.
Life is so promising when ovulation is at its highest
point to fill.
Receive with the intent to conceive... The
conception of love breeds deeply in the womb.
With each stroke, pride grows continuously until
consumed...
Assume the position, return to the throne...
Capitalize specifically on the legacy alone.
You would be amazed at the heritage that's left out
in the cold.
Rejuvenation of your mind is something that is
being prolonged...
I kid you not, I'm not the shit starter with any ill
tensions.
I just want intimacy to really be intimate and truly
enjoy the feeling.
Levels of the healing defined as ultimate
satisfaction.
Knowing the worth in the beginning so in the end
there's no need of asking...
Where do we go from here?
Do you really love me?

Where They At Though

I'm so melodic with words, how can I ever get
curved...
Umph,
unestablished women I suppose... I guess those are
the cards I must fold.
Everything happens for a reason I was told.
Lonely in the bed, a mess of emotions in the head.
Simple busting guts is so boring, where's the
head???
Intimate back rubs and stimulation that led...
To the most enjoyable time you could ask for in
between 5 and 60 minutes.
Whether it's a quickie or
I'm standing up in it. Melodic when I'm hitting it.
Every single note from the throat from the
beginning to the ending.
Dang this chorus is getting it. I love the way it's
sending...
Chills down my spine, so in my mind. So,
intertwined that the beats are off track but I gotta
gud grip from behind.
Steady wit flow, no need of letting go. 'Til that 5, 4,
3...*ahhh* you already know.

Who Going To Stop Us?

When we get the time after all that's said and done, you and I connect beyond spectrums less identified to the young.

Something that only the ones who understand the principles and the dynamic which it's evolved from...

Something far from the wham bam and curiosity of, "Did you cum?"

Something that gets jotted down in the memory to reflect on...

Something that could be justified even though no explanation is ever needed.

Something ever so needed just to justify the emotions in which the actions caused a reaction that left feelings ever so heated.

Believe it... When we connect, they read it.
So obvious to see it, even the blind can peep it.

Agree it's SOOO easy to achieve it. I mean now that we've conceived it, we continue to give life to continue to breed it.

Let it as live as it wants to be free, it's the only reason you are perceived as over the top conceited...

We be it... The connect that sets standards and we connect with no manners.

It's our love and who's gone come stop or handle us???
Nobody!

Who Really Wants To Be Overlooked?

You can work 70 hours a week, be fed good food, clothing, good fabrics, nobody worries about anything getting cut off and still manages to make every function, every practice pick-up.

Everything under the sun to support ya peoples... And somehow, they will still make you feel like you've failed them all.

Because they have no values or morals for what LITTLE they could do to show just the smallest form of appreciation...

Drawing a very fine line as to "what" it means to be a parent, husband, and friend, whatever.

#SocietysfinestIAM where's the heritage and love and respect and responsibilities that are automatically given???

Wiser, Stronger, And Less Tolerant

I need me an old school cutty buddy...

New school snack, futuristic homieloverfriend.

Who knows how to act.

Got my back like Cadillacs and leather seats. Rolling with me like vogues and 84's.

Safe and secure like the vault before the crime... Only opening to "MY" dangerous thoughts in "MY" dangerous mind.

I need a "YOU," do "YOU" have the time???

Invest in stocks and bonds and sit back and watch them climb.

Meeting with account specialists in between the grind... Sipping coffee with bagels on the first floor.

See you tomorrow, cutty buddy, snack, homieloverfriend plus more...

You Must Be Big Mad

If conceited is how you view me, just let me be.

My confidence in who I am helps me sleep. Only you have a problem with how I eat.

Jealousy seems to be how you feed. I love my ways and I'm not the only one who does either.

I've paid my days and laid my nights.

I've earned my title solid, out right.

Conceited is an opinion from others about a person, their ways, and movements.

Just ask me and I'm able to prove shit...

So, I appreciate your views, thoughts, and mental space.

#SocietysfinestIAM forever anyways...

Keep in touch!

@societysfinestiam

@societys finest ent

@societysfinest2